THE CHICAGO BLACKHAWKS

BY

MARK STEWART

CONTENT CONSULTANT
DENIS GIBBONS
SOCIETY FOR INTERNATIONAL HOCKEY RESEARCH

NORWOOD HOUSE PRESS

CHICAGO, ILLINOIS

Norwood House Press
P.O. Box 316598
Chicago, Illinois 60631

For information regarding Norwood House Press, please visit our website at:
www.norwoodhousepress.com or call 866-565-2900.

All photos courtesy of Associated Press except the following:
Diamond Match Co. (6, 34 left), Author's Collection (7, 15, 33, 43 bottom),
Hockey Hall of Fame (8, 27, 36, 39), NHL Action Stamps (9), Chicago Blackhawks (10, 17),
Bee Hive Golden Corn Syrup/Cargill, Inc. (21), Beckett Publications (22, 35 bottom),
Société de Publication Merlin (28), Getty Images (32, 39), Macfadden Publications, Inc. (34 right),
Topps, Inc. (35 top left & right, 37, 38, 40, 42 top, 43 top, 45), McDiarmid/Cartophilium (41),
O-Pee-Chee Ltd. (42 bottom).
Cover Photo: Cal Sport Media via AP Images

The memorabilia and artifacts pictured in this book are presented for educational and informational purposes,
and come from the collection of the author.

Editor: Mike Kennedy
Designer: Ron Jaffe
Project Management: Black Book Partners, LLC.
Special thanks to Topps, Inc.

Library of Congress Cataloging-in-Publication Data

Stewart, Mark, 1960 July 7-
  The Chicago Blackhawks / by Mark Stewart.
      pages cm. -- (Team spirit)
  Includes bibliographical references and index.
  Summary: "A revised Team Spirit Hockey edition featuring the Chicago
Blackhawks that chronicles the history and accomplishments of the team.
Includes access to the Team Spirit website which provides additional
information and photos"-- Provided by publisher.
  ISBN 978-1-59953-617-0 (library edition : alk. paper) -- ISBN
978-1-60357-625-3 (ebook) 1. Chicago Blackhawks (Hockey team)--Juvenile
literature. I. Title.
  GV848.C48S78 2014
  796.962'640977311--dc23
                                                    2013034907

Manufactured in the United States of America in Stevens Point, Wisconsin.
239N—012014

COVER PHOTO: Team Spirit is always in full supply for the Blackhawks.

TABLE OF CONTENTS

R0441879501

ABOUT OUR GLOSSARY

In this book, there may be several words that you are reading for the first time. Some are sports words, some are new vocabulary words, and some are familiar words that are used in an unusual way. All of these words are defined on page 46. Throughout the book, sports words appear in **bold type**. Regular vocabulary words appear in *bold italic type*.

MEET THE BLACKHAWKS

There are many ways to win a championship in the **National Hockey League (NHL)**. Some teams depend on superstars to carry them to victory. Others overwhelm opponents with wave after wave of hardworking skaters. Then there are the unexpected champions—the teams that make fans scratch their heads and wonder: *How did they do that?*

The Chicago Blackhawks have won all three ways. They work wonders with the talent on their **roster** and find ways to succeed that other clubs often overlook. Win or lose, however, the "Hawks" play as hard and as smart as any team in the NHL.

This book tells the story of the Blackhawks. They have had some amazing players and have won some heart-stopping games. The most famous Blackhawks are known for being excellent all-around stars. The team is at its best when each player hopping over the boards is ready to do whatever it takes to win.

Jonathan Toews and Patrick Kane start the attack for the Blackhawks.

GLORY DAYS

The 1920s are sometimes called the "Golden Age of Sports." Sports of all kinds became wildly popular with the public. Athletes became as famous as explorers, movie stars, and military heroes. Unfortunately, **professional** hockey lagged behind other sports. At the dawn of this exciting time, the NHL was based in Canada. American fans were hungry for hockey, but there was no place in the United States to see the NHL teams play.

JOHNNY GOTTSELIG
"Black Hawks"

Many people wondered whether a league that "belonged" to Canada could expand south of the country's border and still call itself national. The NHL was eager to try. It started placing teams in major American cities, including Chicago, Illinois. The Blackhawks played their first season in 1926–27, along with the New York Rangers and Detroit Cougars (who later became the Red Wings).

The Blackhawks had some of the league's top players, including high-scoring Johnny Gottselig and a pesky right wing named Mush March. Goalie Chuck Gardiner was one of the best in the business. This trio led the Blackhawks to the **Stanley Cup** in 1934. Chicago won the championship again four years later. Burly Earl Seibert was a dangerous scorer and played great defense. Mike Karakas starred in goal.

The Blackhawks of the 1930s were unusual because of the number of Americans they had in uniform. Most teams had only one or two players born in the U.S., if any at all. The owner of the Blackhawks, Frederic McLaughlin, wanted to promote American hockey. He signed every U.S. player he could find.

During the 1940s, the Blackhawks were led by several players destined for the **Hall of Fame**, including Bill Mosienko, Clint Smith, and the Bentley brothers, Max and Doug. During the

LEFT: Johnny Gottselig was one of Chicago's first stars.
ABOVE: Team owner Frederic McLaughlin made finding American players a top priority.

1950s, however, Chicago did not record a single winning season. Things began to change when center Stan Mikita, goalie Glenn Hall, and defenseman Pierre Pilote joined the club. In 1960–61, Chicago won its third Stanley Cup.

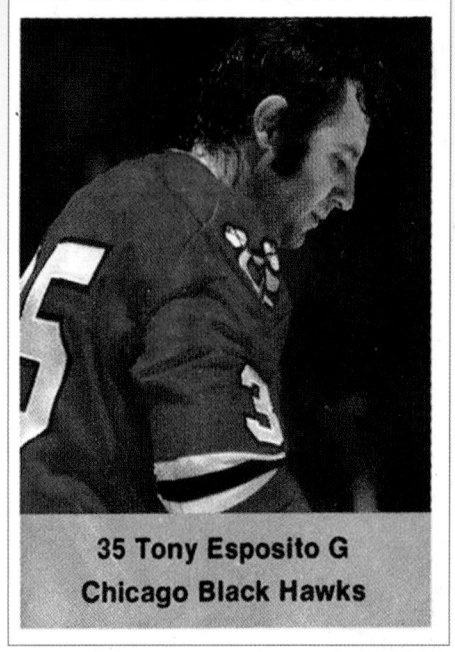

35 Tony Esposito G
Chicago Black Hawks

The team's star of stars was 22-year-old Bobby Hull. Known as the "Golden Jet," he electrified fans. Hull was a lightning-fast skater who never slowed down. He had arms like sledgehammers and a body like an *anvil*. No one could bump him off the puck. Hull's slapshot exploded off his stick at over 110 miles per hour (161 kilometers per hour). If a goalie blinked, the puck was past him!

The Blackhawks returned to the **Stanley Cup Finals** in 1962, 1965, 1971, and 1973. One of their top players in the early 1970s was an acrobatic goalie named Tony Esposito. Along with defensemen Keith Magnuson, Bill White, Pat Stapleton, and Doug Wilson, "Tony O" made Chicago a tough team to score against—and a tough team to beat.

The Blackhawks remained strong during the 1980s. During the *decade*, they reached the finals of their **conference** five times.

LEFT: Bobby Hull earned his nickname the "Golden Jet" because of his speed and blond hair. **ABOVE**: Chicago fans loved to cheer for Tony Esposito.

Unfortunately, Chicago was unable to go all the way and raise the Stanley Cup. It was not for a lack of talent. The Hawks had some of the top players in the NHL during this time, including Denis Savard and Steve Larmer. By the end of the 1980s, the club had added more talented players, such as Dirk Graham, Chris Chelios, Ed Belfour, and Jeremy Roenick. Coach Mike Keenan whipped his squad into shape and led them back to the Stanley Cup Finals in 1992.

Age and injuries prevented the Blackhawks from becoming one of the league's best teams. In the 1997–98 season, Chicago missed the **playoffs** for the first time in 29 years. A once proud team was on the verge of collapse. It would take a new owner, a new attitude, and a load of team spirit to lift the Blackhawks back to the top of the NHL.

In 2007, Rocky Wirtz took over the team from his father, Bill. He made many changes and brought back great players such as Hull and Mikita to work for the team. The Blackhawks began rebuilding with young stars, including Jonathan Toews, Patrick Kane, Patrick Sharp, Corey Crawford, and Duncan Keith.

In no time, the Blackhawks were winning again, and the team's arena was full every night. After years of empty seats, the Blackhawks had the highest attendance in the NHL in 2008–09. The big crowds energized the young players. The addition of goal-scorer Marian Hossa and coach Joel Quenneville gave the Blackhawks experienced leaders who could teach the Hawks how to win. In 2009–10, Chicago beat the Philadelphia Flyers to win its fourth Stanley Cup. Three seasons later, in 2012–13, the Blackhawks did it again. They defeated the Boston Bruins for the fifth championship in team history.

LEFT: Chris Chelios appeared on the cover of the team's media guide in 1997.   **ABOVE**: Michal Rozsival and Duncan Keith exchange high fives with teammates during the 2012–13 season.

HOME ICE

For 70 years, the Blackhawks played their home games in Chicago Stadium. It was a beloved and legendary building. When it opened, Chicago Stadium was the largest indoor arena in the world. It was also the first to have air conditioning, which sometimes created fog over the rink! When the arena was torn down, many people watched the demolition with tears in their eyes.

In 1994, the Blackhawks moved into their current home. The team made sure the arena was a great place to watch a game, just like Chicago Stadium. The *acoustics* were designed to increase the sound of cheers in the building. Statues of Bobby Hull and Stan Mikita stand outside the arena.

BY THE NUMBERS

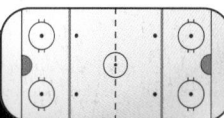

- The Blackhawks' arena has 19,717 seats for hockey.
- It cost $175 million to build in 1994.
- As of 2013, six uniform numbers have been retired by the team: 1 (Glenn Hall), 3 (Pierre Pilote and Keith Magnuson), 9 (Bobby Hull), 18 (Denis Savard), 21 (Stan Mikita), and 35 (Tony Esposito).

The giant video board that hangs over the ice can be seen in this shot of Chicago's arena.

DRESSED FOR SUCCESS

The Blackhawks have always used a *logo* and colors that honor the Native American culture of their home state. Frederic McLaughlin, the man who founded the team, chose the name. It comes from Chief Black Hawk of the Sauk nation. Chicago's logo shows the head of Chief Black Hawk. The team colors are red, black, and white.

The Chicago jersey is worn by fans all over the world, even by people who don't follow hockey. The team's name and logo honor the memory of a heroic leader who fought bravely against the U.S. Army trying to regain the lands of his ancestors.

LEFT: Marian Hossa celebrates a goal in a 2012–13 game wearing the team's away uniform.   **ABOVE**: Harry Watson models the team's home uniform from the 1950s.

WE WON!

The Blackhawks have been Stanley Cup champions in three very different *eras* of pro hockey. Not surprisingly, they won with three very different teams. In the 1933–34 season, Chicago was led by the **line** of Mush March, Doc Romnes, and Paul Thompson—backed by defensemen Sid Abel and Lionel Conacher, and goalie Chuck Gardiner. They faced the Detroit Red Wings in the Stanley Cup Finals, which was a best-of-five series at the time. The Blackhawks won in four games, with two of their victories coming in **overtime**. March fired the shot that sealed the championship in Game 4.

Four years later, the Blackhawks shocked NHL fans by returning to the Stanley Cup Finals. The team had a losing record during the regular season but managed to grab the last playoff spot. Goalie Mike Karakas came alive in the **postseason**, as did the rest of his teammates. The Blackhawks beat the Montreal Canadiens and New York Americans to earn a shot at the mighty Toronto Maple Leafs. Karakas sat out the first two games with a broken toe, and then

The 1961 champs posed with the Stanley Cup for this souvenir photo.

CHICAGO BLACK HAWKS
WORLD CHAMPIONS & STANLEY CUP WINNERS 1960-1961

returned to the ice wearing a special boot. Amazingly, he allowed just two goals in two games as Chicago took the series for its second championship.

There was nothing surprising about the Blackhawks in 1960–61. In an era when the top teams were stocked with future Hall of Famers, Chicago had four all-time greats: goalie Glenn Hall, defenseman Pierre Pilote, and forwards Stan Mikita and Bobby Hull. Led by team captain Ed Litzenberger, the Blackhawks faced Gordie Howe and the Red Wings in the Stanley Cup Finals.

The series was tight from the start. The teams were knotted after four games. In Game 5, the Blackhawks cruised to a 6–3 blowout in front of a stomping, screaming Chicago crowd. In Game 6, Detroit took a 1–0 lead and went on a **power play**. But Chicago **rookie** Reggie Fleming stole a pass meant for Howe and scored a spectacular goal. The Blackhawks went on to win 5–1 and celebrated their third Stanley Cup.

The Chicago teams that won the Stanley Cup in 2010 and 2013 had great heart and wonderful depth at every position. Opponents did not dare relax against the Blackhawks. The club was led by young captain Jonathan Toews, center Patrick Kane, defensive wizard Duncan Keith, and **veteran** goal-scorer Marian Hossa.

In the 2010 Stanley Cup Finals, Chicago did battle with the Philadelphia Flyers. The Blackhawks opened the series with a pair of narrow victories. The Flyers responded with two victories to even things up. Chicago won Game 5 and then captured the Stanley Cup in Game 6 on an overtime goal by Kane. Toews was awarded the Conn Smythe Trophy as the **Most Valuable Player (MVP)** of the playoffs.

Three years later, the Blackhawks finished with the best record in the NHL. They were on fire when the playoffs began. Chicago faced a stiff challenge from the Red Wings in the second round. The Hawks made a brilliant comeback to win the series in seven games.

The Blackhawks were ready for anything as they faced the Boston Bruins in the Stanley Cup Finals. Boston outskated Chicago early in the series and won two of the first three games. An overtime goal by

defenseman Brent Seabrook tied the series and gave the Blackhawks a huge boost. They won Game 5, and then won the Stanley Cup in Game 6 on goals by Bryan Bickell and Dave Bolland.

The finish was all the more incredible because Bickell and Bolland scored just 17 seconds apart with less then two minutes left in the game. The Boston crowd sat in stunned silence as the Hawks celebrated their fifth championship. It was hockey the "Chicago way." Seabrook, Bickell, and Bolland had combined for only 24 goals during the regular season, but they played like champions when it mattered the most.

LEFT: Jonathan Toews raises the Stanley Cup after Chicago's championship in 2010.   **ABOVE**: The Hawks rush to congratulate Brent Seabrook after his game-winning goal in the 2013 Stanley Cup Finals.

GO-TO GUYS

To be a true star in the NHL, you need more than a great slapshot. You have to be a "go-to guy"—someone teammates trust to make the winning play when the seconds are ticking away in a big game. Blackhawks fans have had a lot to cheer about over the years, including these great stars.

THE PIONEERS

PIERRE PILOTE   Defenseman

• BORN: 12/11/1931 • PLAYED FOR TEAM: 1955–56 TO 1967–68

Pierre "Pete" Pilote loved to deliver crushing **hip-checks** that sent fast-skating forwards spinning down the ice. Pilote also handled the puck extremely well. He teamed with Elmer Vasko to form the league's best defensive duo in the early 1960s.

GLENN HALL   Goalie

• BORN: 10/3/1931 • PLAYED FOR TEAM: 1957–58 TO 1966–67

Glenn Hall helped introduce a new style of goaltending. He would often leave the net to cut down a shooter's angle or retrieve a loose puck. In addition, Hall was almost indestructible. He played 502 games in a row for the Blackhawks.

BOBBY HULL   Left Wing

- BORN: 1/3/1939   • PLAYED FOR TEAM: 1957–58 TO 1971–72

Few players were faster or stronger than Bobby Hull. He also had the hardest slapshot in the game—maybe the hardest ever. Hull led the NHL in goals seven times. His brother, Dennis, played for Chicago and also had a great slapshot.

STAN MIKITA   Center

- BORN: 5/20/1940
- PLAYED FOR TEAM: 1958–59 TO 1979–80

If an opponent had a weakness, Stan Mikita would find it. Mikita was a lumbering skater, but he was a skilled passer and shooter, and his ability to out-think opponents was legendary. Mikita was one of the first players to master the art of shooting with a curved stick.

TONY ESPOSITO   Goalie

- BORN: 4/23/1943
- PLAYED FOR TEAM: 1969–70 TO 1983–84

As a rookie, Tony Esposito set a record with 15 **shutouts** and led the Blackhawks to the playoffs. For the next 13 years, it was the same story—Tony O was between the pipes, and Chicago made the postseason. His flop-to-the-ice style was copied by a *generation* of netminders.

ABOVE: Stan Mikita

DENIS SAVARD   Center

- BORN: 2/4/1961
- PLAYED FOR TEAM: 1980–81 TO 1989–90 & 1994–95 TO 1996–97

Denis Savard scored 30 or more goals for Chicago seven years in a row. His favorite move was the "Spin-O-Rama"—Savard would catch the defense off-guard by spinning completely around and then surprising the goalie with a shot.

STEVE LARMER   Right Wing

- BORN: 6/16/1961   • PLAYED FOR TEAM: 1980–81 TO 1992–93

No Chicago player was better at creating scoring opportunities than

Steve Larmer. He won the Calder Trophy as the league's top rookie and scored more than 30 goals nine times in 11 seasons for the Blackhawks.

JEREMY ROENICK   Center

- BORN: 1/17/1970
- PLAYED FOR TEAM: 1988–89 TO 1995–96

Chicago fans loved Jeremy Roenick as much for his goal scoring as they did for his funny and outrageous personality. Roenick topped 100 points (goals plus **assists**) three times for the Blackhawks and played in the **All-Star Game** four times.

CHRIS CHELIOS — Defenseman

- BORN 1/25/1962   • PLAYED FOR TEAM: 1990–91 TO 1998–99

After trading for Chris Chelios, the Blackhawks rose to the top of the **standings** for the first time since the 1960s. Opponents rarely challenged him—in one-on-one battles, he won almost every time. Chelios was voted into the Hall of Fame in 2013.

DUNCAN KEITH — Defenseman

- BORN: 7/16/1983   • FIRST SEASON WITH TEAM: 2005–06

If the Blackhawks had to shut down one opponent, that assignment went to Duncan Keith. His combination of scoring and defense helped Chicago win the Stanley Cup in 2010 and again in 2013.

JONATHAN TOEWS — Center

- BORN: 4/29/1988   • FIRST SEASON WITH TEAM: 2007–08

The Blackhawks chose Jonathan Toews with the third pick in the 2006 NHL **draft**. In 2008, he became the third-youngest player in league history to be named a team captain. Toews won the Conn Smythe Trophy in 2010.

PATRICK KANE — Right Wing

- BORN: 11/19/1988   • FIRST SEASON WITH TEAM: 2007–08

In 2007, the Blackhawks had the top pick in the NHL draft for the first time ever. They chose Patrick Kane. He won the Calder Trophy as the league's top rookie in 2007–08 and led Chicago to two championships in the years that followed.

LEFT: Jeremy Roenick

CALLING THE SHOTS

When a team has been around as long as the Blackhawks, it is no surprise that some of the sport's best coaches have stood behind the bench for them. Among the most successful were Tommy Gorman, Bill Stewart, and Rudy Pilous. Each guided the Blackhawks to the Stanley Cup.

Another important figure in the club's history was Tommy Ivan. He came to Chicago in 1954 after leading the Detroit Red Wings to three Stanley Cups. Ivan coached the team and then became its **general manager**. He did a magnificent job rebuilding the club that Pilous guided to the championship.

The coach who logged the most seasons in Chicago was Billy Reay. He took over the team in 1963–64 and stayed until the late 1970s—14 years in all. Reay had just one losing season during that time. He led the Blackhawks to the Stanley Cup Finals three times.

Mike Keenan was just as famous—and successful—as the coach of the Hawks. Keenan was super-tough. When he arrived in Chicago in 1988, the Blackhawks were a losing team. Keenan turned them into a

Joel Quenneville hugs Dave Bolland after Chicago's 2013 championship.

Stanley Cup **contender**. He coached Chicago to the conference finals in each of his first two seasons. In his fourth and last season, "Iron Mike" led Chicago all the way to the Stanley Cup Finals.

The coach who brought glory back to the Blackhawks was Joel Quenneville—or "Coach Q" to his players. Quenneville came to Chicago as a scout in 2008, but he was promoted to coach at the end of the 2008–09 season. A year later, the Blackhawks hoisted the Stanley Cup for the first time since 1961. Coach Q led the team to another Stanley Cup in 2013.

APRIL 5, 1938

Things were not looking good for the Blackhawks as they prepared for the 1938 Stanley Cup Finals against the Toronto Maple Leafs. Chicago reached the championship round with surprising victories in its first two playoff series. But those wins came at a high cost. Goalie Mike Karakas broke a toe and was in great pain. With Game 1 in Toronto approaching, his foot was so swollen that he could not even put on his skate.

NHL teams did not carry extra goalies in the 1930s. The rules stated that a team with an injured goalie could find a replacement, as long as the opponent agreed. Davey Kerr of the New York Rangers happened to be in the crowd at Maple Leaf Gardens that night and offered to play for Chicago. But Conn Smythe—the man who ran the Maple Leafs—refused. Instead, he told the Blackhawks that they had to use a Toronto **minor leaguer** named Alfie Moore.

Moore's nickname was "Half-Pint" because he stood barely over five feet tall. As Moore suited up, he apologized to his new teammates

Mike Karakas shows the form that made him one of
Chicago's all-time best goalies.

and admitted that they got a bad deal. When he saw Smythe before
the game, he shouted, "I hope I stop every puck you fellows fire at
me—even if I have to eat the rubber!"

Smythe did not know it, but he had **unleashed** a wildcat. After
allowing an early goal to Toronto, Moore stopped every shot he faced.
Meanwhile, Johnny Gottselig scored twice and Paul Thompson
added another goal to give Chicago a 3–1 victory. After the game,
the Maple Leafs were stunned, while the Blackhawks were full of
confidence. When Karakas returned to the ice, they went on to win
the Stanley Cup.

LEGEND HAS IT

SPORTS *Le* HOCKEY *et ses vedettes* 25¢

Vol. 2 — No 3   DECEMBRE 1963

WAS STANISLAV GVOTH THE BLACKHAWKS' TOP CAREER SCORER?

LEGEND HAS IT that he was. Of course, Chicago fans know him as Stan Mikita. In 1948, when the Soviet Union's army seized control of Czechoslovakia, Mikita's parents sent him to live with his aunt and uncle in Canada. The eight-year-old took the name of his relatives, Mikita. He ended his career with 1,467 points—more than anyone else in team history.

ABOVE: Stan Mikita poses for the cover of a French-language hockey magazine from the 1960s. His real name was Stanislav Gvoth.

DID THE BLACKHAWKS ONCE LOSE TO A ROCK BAND?

LEGEND HAS IT that they did. In 1977, the Hawks were supposed to host a playoff game against the New York Islanders in early April, but the rock band Led Zeppelin was booked for the arena the same night. The two teams ended up moving the game to the Islanders' home ice in New York. Even that was difficult. Before they could use the arena, the Islanders had to buy out all the tickets for the Bugs Bunny Easter Show! Chicago's season ended that night with a 2–1 loss.

DID THREE BROTHERS EVER PLAY TOGETHER ON THE SAME LINE?

LEGEND HAS IT that they did. On New Year's Day in 1943, Max, Doug, and Reg Bentley skated together against the New York Rangers. It was the first time an "all-brothers" line took the ice in an NHL game. Chicago won 6–5, but the "Bentley" experiment soon ended, and the line was broken up.

One of the great pieces of Chicago sports *memorabilia* is the puck that won the 2010 Stanley Cup for the Blackhawks. It ended 49 years of frustration and set the team on a path to become a modern NHL *dynasty*. Just one problem—no one knows where that puck is!

The Hawks faced the Philadelphia Flyers in Chicago in Game 6 with a chance to win the Stanley Cup. With the score tied 3–3 in overtime, Patrick Kane slammed a shot past goalie Michael Leighton. The puck buried itself in the padding at the back of the net. Kane and Jonathan Toews started celebrating, but no one else knew what happened. The goal judge didn't even turn the light on. Only after a video review was it ruled a goal.

What happened next is a mystery. During the victory celebration, linesman Steve Miller dislodged the puck, picked it up, and skated off the ice. He handed it off to someone, but to this day he doesn't remember who that person was. The puck was never seen again. The NHL was very upset and actually suspended Miller briefly.

Patrick Kane leaps into the arms of Antti Niemi after his championship goal was ruled good by officials.

Meanwhile, the search continued. A Chicago restaurant even offered a $50,000 reward for the missing puck. Was it stolen? Perhaps. However, it is just as likely that the person who got the puck from Miller didn't know it was *the* puck. Which means it might be sitting in a shoebox or in a junk drawer somewhere in Chicago ... or maybe being knocked around a frozen pond by some kids pretending it's overtime in Game 6. How funny would that be?

TEAM SPIRIT

Chicago hockey fans are some of the loudest and proudest on the planet. When the Blackhawks score, the crowd shakes the building with its cheers. The team's new arena was actually built in a way that *amplifies* the noise. That arena is also one of the largest in the NHL. Chicago is one of the few teams that averages more than 20,000 fans a game.

Many fan *traditions* remain from the team's old home, Chicago Stadium. Perhaps the best is the loud pipe organ that plays during games. When the music starts, so does Tommy Hawk, the team's mascot. Tommy is a giant hawk that roams through the stands wearing a Chicago jersey. If Tommy thinks fans are too laid-back, look out—he will give them a Silly String shower!

LEFT: Tommy Hawk gets the fans fired up during a game that was played outside at Chicago's Wrigley Field.
RIGHT: Fans wore this pin during the 1960s.

TIMELINE

The hockey season is played from October through June. That means each season takes place at the end of one year and the beginning of the next. In this timeline, the accomplishments of the Blackhawks are shown by season.

1933–34
The Blackhawks win their first Stanley Cup.

1953–54
Goalie Al Rollins wins the Hart Trophy as the NHL MVP.

1926–27
The Blackhawks play their first season.

1942–43
Doug Bentley is the team's first scoring champion.

1946–47
Max Bentley wins his second scoring title in a row.

Mush March starred for the 1934 champs.

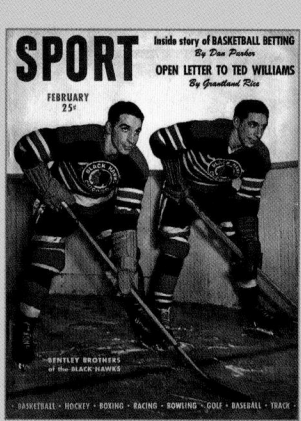

Doug and Max Bentley were front-page news during the 1940s.

Bobby Hull

Doug Wilson

1965–66
Bobby Hull scores 54 goals.

1981–82
Doug Wilson wins the Norris Trophy as the NHL's top defenseman.

2009–10
The team wins its first NHL title in 49 years.

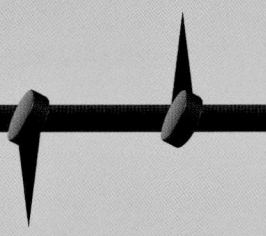

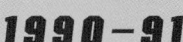

1960–61
Chicago wins its third Stanley Cup.

1990–91
Ed Belfour wins the **Vezina Trophy**.

2012–13
The Blackhawks win their fifth Stanley Cup.

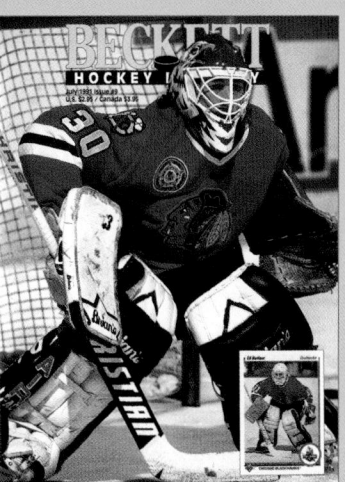

Ed Belfour

FUN FACTS

JUST ONE WORD

For most of the team's history, its name was usually spelled as two words: Black Hawks. In 1986, officials discovered original papers from 1926 that had the name written out as one word. Since then, the team name has been spelled Blackhawks.

STORY TELLER

No Blackhawk disliked training camp more than goalie Glenn Hall. He was late to report almost every year. The excuse he always gave was, "I haven't finished painting my barn."

HANDS UP

Before Billy Reay coached the Blackhawks, he was already famous for something players now do every day. Reay was the first player to thrust his arms in the air after a goal.

SAY CHEESE!

Elmer Vasko might have been the luckiest Blackhawk in history. He never lost any of his teeth during his NHL career, despite the lack of mouthguards or helmets in his playing days.

ELMER VASKO
CHICAGO BLACK HAWKS DEFENSE

PERFECT 10

In 2013, backup goalie Ray Emery set an NHL record by winning his first 10 games of the season. He finished the year with a record of 17–1.

SUCH GENTLEMEN

In 1944–45, Bill Mosienko and Clint Smith had 54 points each. Neither player spent a minute in the penalty box that season.

MUSIC MAN

One of the most beloved Blackhawks never skated for the team. Al Melgard, the organist at Chicago Stadium, entertained fans for four decades starting in the 1930s. He got the job after impressing the team with his quick thinking. Melgard stopped a riot at a boxing match by playing *The Star Spangled Banner*.

LEFT: Earl Seibert wears a jersey showing the team name as Black Hawks.
ABOVE: Smile, Elmer!

DENIS SAVARD • C

"If I see that our losing is being accepted without a fight, I go nuts."

▶ **JEREMY ROENICK,** *on his reputation for "blowing up" at his teammates*

"It doesn't matter how many goals you get or how many points. One-on-one doesn't win the Cup. And that's what you play for."

▶ **DENIS SAVARD,** *on the importance of unselfish play*

"Normally, you try to ignore the crowd reaction. But in Chicago, it's impossible. You can't help but get a lift from it."

▶ **BOBBY HULL,** *on the noise level in old Chicago Stadium*

"That whole season was something special—both for the Blackhawks and for me personally."

▶ **TONY ESPOSITO,** *on his amazing rookie year in 1969–70*

"I can't believe this just happened. It's something you dream of as a kid. To score the winning goal in the Stanley Cup Finals, it was just unbelievable."

▶ **PATRICK KANE,** *on his goal that won the 2010 Stanley Cup*

"I'm the kind of guy who wants the puck, who can make my teammates better."

▶ **JONATHAN TOEWS,** *on his ability as a leader*

LEFT: Denis Savard
ABOVE: Patrick Kane and Jonathan Toews

GREAT DEBATES

People who root for the Blackhawks love to compare their favorite moments, teams, and players. Some debates have been going on for years! How would you settle these classic hockey arguments?

TONY ESPOISTO HAD THE FINEST SEASON OF ANY ROOKIE IN TEAM HISTORY ...

... because he was the top goalie in the NHL in his first year. In 1969–70, Esposito used his acrobatic, flopping style to confuse opponents and make one incredible save after another. Tony O allowed just 2.18 goals per game and set a modern record with 15 shutouts. He not only won the Calder Trophy, he took home the Vezina Trophy, too.

NO CHICAGO ROOKIE WAS MORE "CLUTCH" THAN STEVE LARMER ...

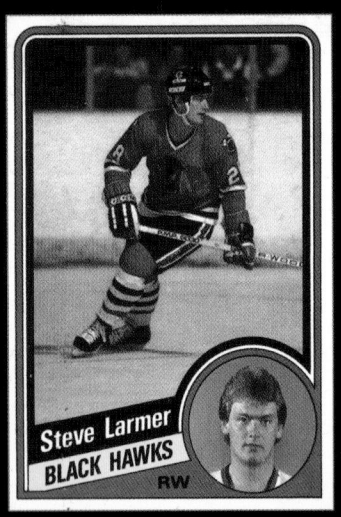

Steve Larmer
BLACK HAWKS
RW

... because he did more than stop goals in close games—he scored goals in close games. In 1982–83, Larmer (LEFT) netted nine game-winning goals for the Hawks. Not only did that help the team finish in first place, it set an NHL record for rookies. Larmer was a right wing with a left-handed shot, which often caught goalies by surprise. It was no surprise when he won the Calder Trophy.

BILL MOSIENKO'S 21-SECOND HAT TRICK WAS THE MOST AMAZING MOMENT IN TEAM HISTORY ...

... because no one has ever come close to scoring three goals that quickly. Mosienko (RIGHT) did it in the final game of the 1951–52 season. He was fourth in the league in goals when the game started. He was second when the game ended. Best of all, the Blackhawks won 7–6.

TWO GOALS IN 17 SECONDS BEATS THREE IN 21 SECONDS ...

... because those two goals won the 2013 Stanley Cup. With less than two minutes left in Game 6, the Boston Bruins led the Blackhawks 2–1. Chicago pulled goalie Corey Crawford and moments later Bryan Bickell tied the game. Everyone thought the game was headed to overtime, but before Boston knew what happened, Dave Bolland fired the Cup-winning shot into the net 17 seconds later.

The great Blackhawks teams and players have left their marks on the record books. These are the "best of the best" …

ALL-TIME GREATS

CHUCK GARDINER

Chuck Gardiner

CHRIS CHELIOS DEFENSE • DÉFENSEUR

Chris Chelios

BLACKHAWKS AWARD WINNERS

HART MEMORIAL TROPHY
MOST VALUABLE PLAYER (MVP)

Max Bentley	1945–46
Al Rollins	1953–54
Bobby Hull	1964–65
Bobby Hull	1965–66
Stan Mikita	1966–67
Stan Mikita	1967–68

CALDER TROPHY
TOP ROOKIE

Cully Dahlstrom	1937–38
Ed Litzenberger	1954–55
Red Hay	1959–60
Tony Esposito	1969–70
Steve Larmer	1982–83
Ed Belfour	1990–91
Patrick Kane	2007–08

CONN SMYTHE TROPHY
MVP DURING PLAYOFFS

Jonathan Toews	2009–10
Patrick Kane	2012–13

ART ROSS TROPHY
TOP SCORER

Roy Conacher	1948–49
Bobby Hull	1959–60
Bobby Hull	1961–62
Stan Mikita	1963–64
Stan Mikita	1964–65
Bobby Hull	1965–66
Stan Mikita	1966–67
Stan Mikita	1967–68

VEZINA TROPHY
TOP GOALTENDER

Chuck Gardiner	1931–32
Chuck Gardiner	1933–34
Lorne Chabot	1934–35
Glenn Hall	1962–63
Glenn Hall*	1966–67
Denis DeJordy	1966–67
Tony Esposito	1969–70
Tony Esposito & Gary Smith	1971–72
Tony Esposito*	1973–74
Ed Belfour	1990–91
Ed Belfour	1992–93

JAMES NORRIS MEMORIAL TROPHY
TOP DEFENSEMAN

Pierre Pilote	1962–63
Pierre Pilote	1963–64
Pierre Pilote	1964–65
Doug Wilson	1981–82
Chris Chelios	1992–93
Chris Chelios	1995–96
Duncan Keith	2009–10

ALL-STAR GAME MVP

Bobby Hull	1969–70
Bobby Hull	1970–71
Eric Daze	2001–02
Patrick Sharp	2010–11

* Shared the award with another player.

BLACKHAWKS ACHIEVEMENTS

ACHIEVEMENT	YEAR
Stanley Cup Finalists	1930–31
Stanley Cup Champions	1933–34
Stanley Cup Champions	1937–38
Stanley Cup Finalists	1943–44
Stanley Cup Champions	1960–61
Stanley Cup Finalists	1961–62
Stanley Cup Finalists	1964–65
Stanley Cup Finalists	1970–71
Stanley Cup Finalists	1972–73
Stanley Cup Finalists	1991–92
Stanley Cup Champions	2009–10
Stanley Cup Champions	2012–13

BLACK HAWKS

BILLY REAY   coach

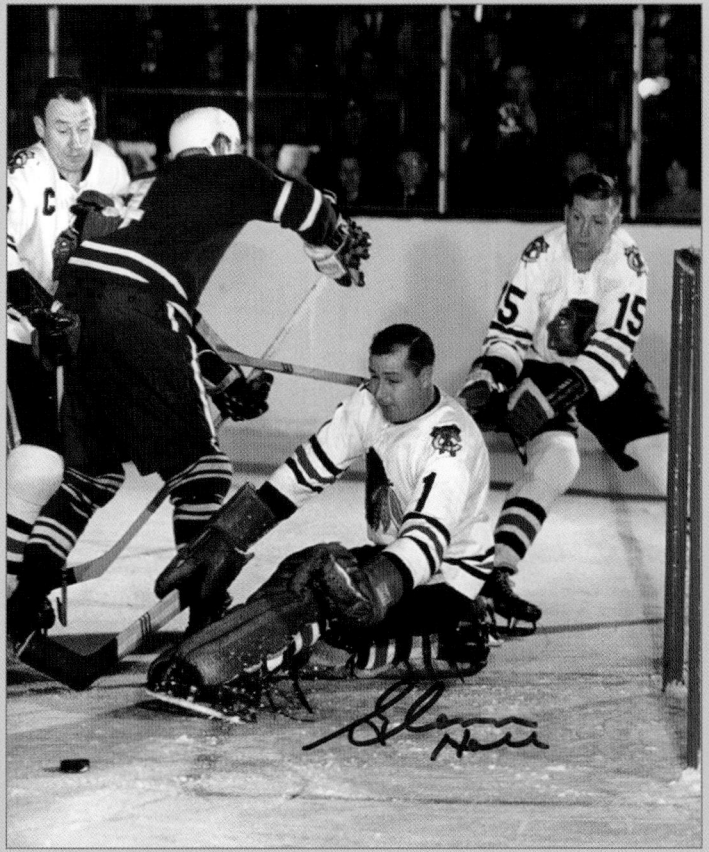

ABOVE: Billy Reay was one of the best coaches in team history. He led the Hawks to the Stanley Cup Finals in 1965, 1971, and 1973. **LEFT**: Glenn Hall makes a save. He signed this photo after his playing days were over.

PINPOINTS

The history of a hockey team is made up of many smaller stories. These stories take place all over the map—not just in the city a team calls "home." Match the pushpins on these maps to the **TEAM FACTS**, and you will begin to see the story of the Blackhawks unfold!

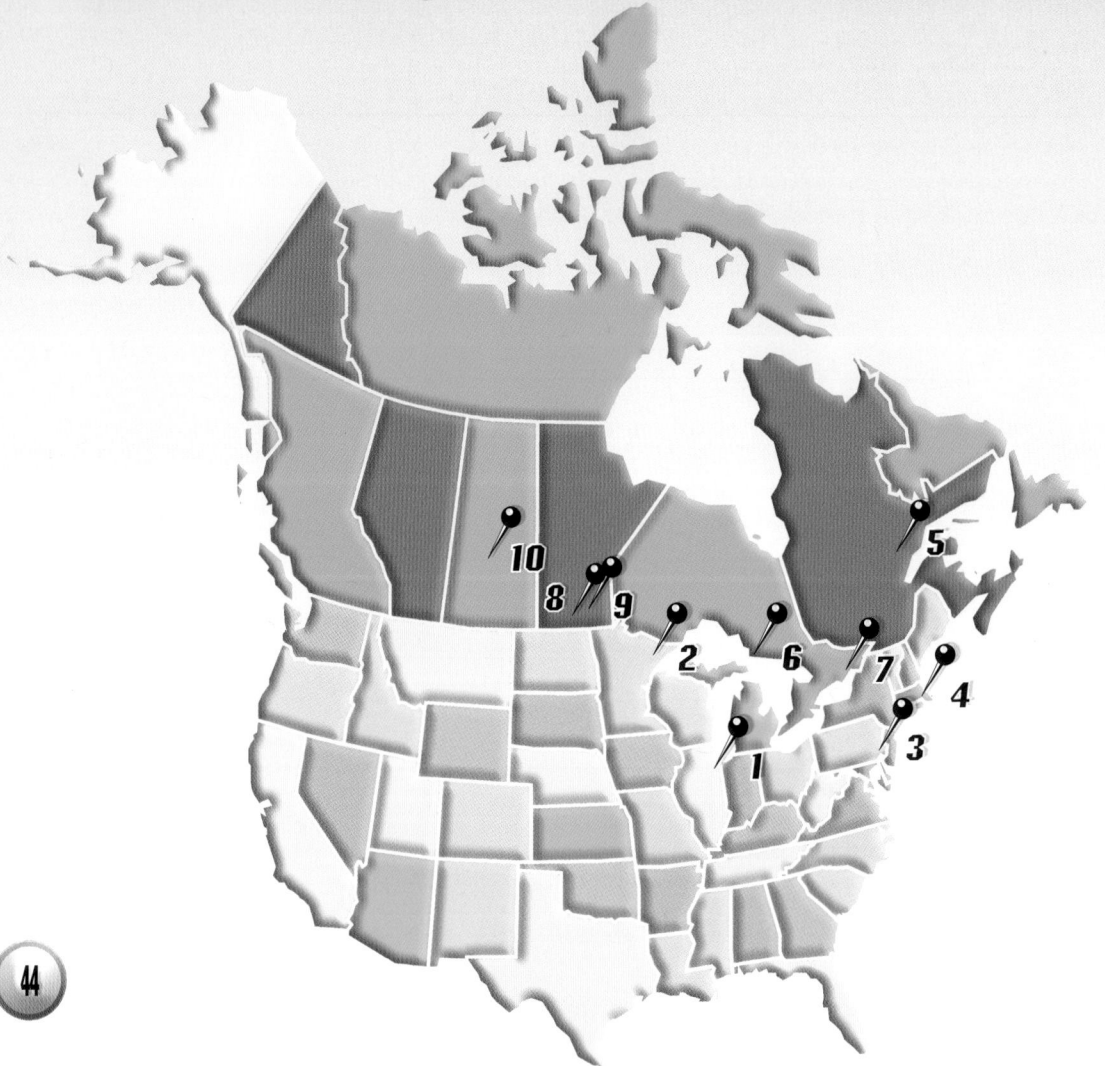

TEAM FACTS

1   Chicago, Illinois—*The Blackhawks have played here since 1926.*

2   Aurora, Minnesota—*Mike Karakas was born here.*

3   Philadelphia, Pennsylvania—*The Blackhawks won the 2010 Stanley Cup here.*

4   Boston, Massachusetts—*Jeremy Roenick was born here.*

5   Kenogami, Quebec—*Pierre Pilote was born here.*

6   Sault Ste. Marie, Ontario—*Tony Esposito was born here.*

7   Pointe Ann, Ontario—*Bobby and Dennis Hull were born here.*

8   Carman, Manitoba—*Ed Belfour was born here.*

9   Winnipeg, Manitoba—*Bill Mosienko was born here.*

10   Humboldt, Saskatchewan—*Glenn Hall was born here.*

11   Edinburgh, Scotland—*Chuck Gardiner was born here.*

12   Sokolce, Slovakia—*Stan Mikita was born here.*

Dennis Hull

GLOSSARY

🧠 *ACOUSTICS*—The volume and quality of sound.

🏒 **ALL-STAR GAME**—The annual game that features the best players from the NHL.

🧠 *AMPLIFIES*—Increases.

🧠 *ANVIL*—A heavy iron block.

🏒 **ASSISTS**—Passes that lead to a goal.

🏒 **CONFERENCE**—A large group of teams. There are two conferences in the NHL, and each season each conference sends a team to the Stanley Cup Finals.

🧠 *CONTENDER*—A team that competes for a championship.

🧠 *DECADE*—A period of 10 years; also specific periods, such as the 1950s.

🏒 **DRAFT**—The annual meeting during which NHL teams pick the top high school, college, and international players.

🧠 *DYNASTY*—A family, group, or team that maintains power over time.

🧠 *ERAS*—Periods of time in history.

🏒 **GENERAL MANAGER**—The person who makes business decisions for a team.

🧠 *GENERATION*—A period of years roughly equal to the time it takes for a person to be born, grow up, and have children.

🏒 **HALL OF FAME**—The museum in Toronto, Canada, where hockey's best players are honored. A player voted into the Hall of Fame is sometimes called a "Hall of Famer."

🏒 **HIP-CHECKS**—Body blows using the hip.

🏒 **LINE**—The trio made up by a left wing, center, and right wing.

🧠 *LOGO*—A symbol or design that represents a company or team.

🧠 *MEMORABILIA*—Things collected because of their historical value.

🏒 **MINOR LEAGUER**—A player from one of the professional leagues that operate below the NHL.

🏒 **MOST VALUABLE PLAYER (MVP)**—The award given each year to the league's best player; also given to the best player in the playoffs and All-Star Game.

🏒 **NATIONAL HOCKEY LEAGUE (NHL)**—The professional league that has been operating since 1917.

🏒 **OVERTIME**— An extra period played when a game is tied after three periods. In the NHL playoffs, teams continue to play overtime periods until a goal is scored.

🏒 **PLAYOFFS**—The games played after the season to determine the league champion.

🏒 **POSTSEASON**—Another term for playoffs.

🏒 **POWER PLAY**—A game situation in which one team has at least one extra skater on the ice. A power play occurs when a player commits a penalty and is sent to the penalty box.

🧠 **PROFESSIONAL**—A player or team that plays a sport for money.

🏒 **ROOKIE**—A player in his first year.

🏒 **ROSTER**—The list of a team's active players.

🏒 **SHUTOUTS**—Games in which a team doesn't score a goal.

🏒 **STANDINGS**—A daily list of teams, starting with the team with the best record and ending with the team with the worst record.

🏒 **STANLEY CUP**—The trophy presented to the NHL champion. The first Stanley Cup was awarded in 1893.

🏒 **STANLEY CUP FINALS**—The final playoff series that determines the winner of the Stanley Cup.

🧠 *TRADITIONS*—Beliefs or customs that are handed down from generation to generation.

🧠 *UNLEASHED*—Let loose.

🏒 **VETERAN**—A player with great experience.

🏒 **VEZINA TROPHY**—The annual award given to the NHL's best goalie.

LINE CHANGE

TEAM SPIRIT introduces a great way to stay up to date with your team! Visit our **LINE CHANGE** link and get connected to the latest and greatest updates. **LINE CHANGE** serves as a young reader's ticket to an exclusive web page—with more stories, fun facts, team records, and photos of the Blackhawks. Content is updated during and after each season. The **LINE CHANGE** feature also enables readers to send comments and letters to the author! Log onto:

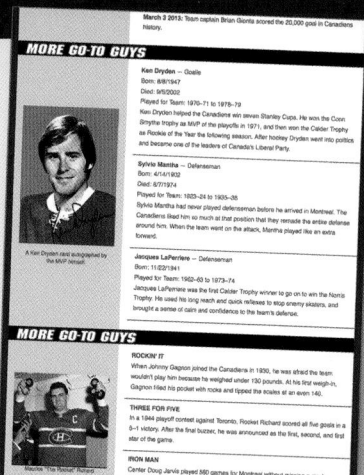

www.norwoodhousepress.com/library.aspx

and click on the tab: **TEAM SPIRIT** to access **LINE CHANGE**.

Read all the books in the series to learn more about professional sports. For a complete listing of the baseball, basketball, football, and hockey teams in the **TEAM SPIRIT** series, visit our website at:

www.norwoodhousepress.com/library.aspx

ON THE ROAD

CHICAGO BLACKHAWKS
1901 West Madison Street
Chicago, Illinois   60612
(312) 455-7000
http://blackhawks.nhl.com

HOCKEY HALL OF FAME
Brookfield Place
30 Yonge Street
Toronto, Ontario, Canada M5E 1X8
(416) 360-7765
http://www.hhof.com

ON THE BOOKSHELF

To learn more about the sport of hockey, look for these books at your library or bookstore:

- Cameron, Steve. *Hockey Hall of Fame Treasures.* Richmond Hill, Ontario, Canada: Firefly Books, 2011.

- MacDonald, James. *Hockey Skills: How to Play Like a Pro.* Berkeley Heights, New Jersey: Enslow Elementary, 2009.

- Keltie, Thomas. *Inside Hockey! The legends, facts, and feats that made the game.* Toronto, Ontario, Canada: Maple Tree Press, 2008.

INDEX

PAGE NUMBERS IN **BOLD** REFER TO ILLUSTRATIONS.

THE TEAM

MARK STEWART has written over 200 books for kids—and more than a dozen books on hockey, including a history of the Stanley Cup and an authorized biography of goalie Martin Brodeur. He grew up in New York City during the 1960s rooting for the Rangers, but has gotten to know a couple of New Jersey Devils, so he roots for a shootout when these teams play each other. Mark comes from a family of writers. His grandfather was Sunday Editor of *The New York Times*, and his mother was Articles Editor of *Ladies' Home Journal* and *McCall's*. Mark has profiled hundreds of athletes over the past 25 years. He has also written several books about his native New York and New Jersey, his home today. Mark is a graduate of Duke University, with a degree in history. He lives and works in a home overlooking Sandy Hook, New Jersey. You can contact Mark through the Norwood House Press website.

DENIS GIBBONS is a writer and editor with *The Hockey News* and a former newsletter editor of the Toronto-based Society for International Hockey Research (SIHR). He was a contributing writer to the publication *Kings of the Ice: A History of World Hockey* and has worked as chief hockey researcher at five Winter Olympics for the ABC, CBS, and NBC television networks. Denis also has worked as a researcher for the FOX Sports Network during the Stanley Cup playoffs. He resides in Burlington, Ontario, Canada with his wife Chris.